W9-CUY-843

ON A MISSION

Bomb Squad Technician

Border Security

Dogs on Patrol

FBI Agent

Fighter Pilot

Firefighter

Paramedic

Search and Rescue Team

Secret Service Agent

Special Forces

SWAT Team

Undercover Police Officer

ON A MISSION

SWAT Team

By John Perritano

Mason Crest
450 Parkway Drive, Suite D
Broomall, PA 19008
www.masoncrest.com

Printed and bound in the United States of America.

Series 978-1-4222-3391-7
Hardback ISBN: 978-1-4222-3402-0
EBook ISBN: 978-1-4222-8511-4

First printing
1 3 5 7 9 8 6 4 2

Produced by Shoreline Publishing Group LLC
Santa Barbara, California
Editorial Director: James Buckley Jr.
Designer: Bill Madrid
Production: Sandy Gordon
www.shorelinepublishing.com
Cover image: MIke Eliason/Santa Barbara County Sheriff's Department

Library of Congress Cataloging-in-Publication Data
Perritano, John.
SWAT team / by John Perritano.
pages cm. -- (On a mission!)
Includes index.
ISBN 978-1-4222-3402-0 (hardback) -- ISBN 978-1-4222-3391-7 (series) -- ISBN 978-1-4222-8511-4 (ebook)
1. Police--Special weapons and tactics units--Juvenile literature. I. Title.
HV8080.S64P476 2016
363.2'3--dc23

2015009748

363.23
PER

Contents

Key Icons to Look For

Words to Understand: These words with their easy-to-understand definitions will increase the reader's understanding of the text, while building vocabulary skills.

Sidebars: This boxed material within the main text allows readers to build knowledge, gain insights, explore possibilities, and broaden their perspectives by weaving together additional information to provide realistic and holistic perspectives.

Research Projects: Readers are pointed toward areas of further inquiry connected to each chapter. Suggestions are provided for projects that encourage deeper research and analysis.

Text-Dependent Questions: These questions send the reader back to the text for more careful attention to the evidence presented here.

Series Glossary of Key Terms: This back-of-the-book glossary contains terminology used throughout this series. Words found here increase the reader's ability to read and comprehend higher-level books and articles in this field.

Emergency!

SWAT teams go into situations that might turn deadly at any moment.

6

He was a quiet man, a graphic artist who kept mostly to himself. He worked at a local college. He exercised and was never in trouble. He took his elderly mother to doctor's appointments and helped her run errands. He was a good son.

That's what his neighbors said.

Still, there was another side to Pedro Vargas. The 42-year-old man from Hialeah, Florida, didn't have many friends in the apartment complex where he lived. Some say he was abusive. He'd yell at his mother. All that could not prepare Vargas's neighbors for what happened on one hot July day.

At around 6:30 P.M. on July 26, Vargas poured a flammable liquid on $10,000 in cash. He then set the money ablaze in his fourth-floor apartment. As the money burned, Vargas went on a rampage.

The building's manager and wife ran to the smoke-filled apartment to see what was wrong. Vargas shot them. Vargas then went onto the balcony and fired 20 shots into the street, killing a man. He then

Words to Understand

casings parts of a bullet that remain after a round has been fired

command post field headquarters for commanders during a police operation

deployment positioning resources so they can be ready for action

dispatcher person who sends police personnel to their calls

meandered wandered slowly

tactics organizing and moving forces in battle to achieve an immediate goal ran to apartment 304 and killed its three occupants. Police quickly responded. A gunfight broke out. Vargas scrambled to another apartment— No. 523—and took two people hostage.

The Call Goes Out

"All available officers!"

That's all Andrés López-Cao, a Hialeah police sergeant, heard. A long day was about to get longer. Like all good cops, though, López-Cao turned up the radio when the call went out. "All available officers," the **dispatcher** said again.

López-Cao had already changed out of his uniform for the night. Now, it was time to go back to work as a member of the city's SWAT unit. SWAT stands for Special Weapons and **Tactics**. These highly trained specialists are called out for situations just like this one. López-Cao put his uniform back on, kissed his wife and daughters goodbye, and went out the door.

Luis Garcia also heard the call. He was on his way to the scene of the shootings when he crashed his police SUV. He wasn't hurt. Still, he had to find a way to get to the apartment building where Vargas lived. He called his wife.

"When she arrived, I put my bulletproof vest and my rifles in her car and left immediately," Garcia told the *Miami Herald*. "Despite everything, I had to go to the shooting scene as soon as possible."

Where Is Vargas?

Police had already set up a **command post** by the time Garcia, López-Cao, and the other SWAT team members arrived. As commanders discussed their next move, police looked down from a helicopter that hovered overhead. Vargas wasn't on the roof. No one knew where he was.

Members of the SWAT team, Garcia and López-Cao included, suited up. They put on their body armor and made sure their weapons were loaded. SWAT commander Hubert Ruiz was puzzled. Where could Vargas be hiding?

When SWAT teams assemble for an assignment, they always meet to coordinate their efforts.

If technology can save lives, SWAT teams are all for it. Sometimes, they send a camera-equipped robot into a danger zone to show officers the way.

Ruiz ordered his unit to go through the building as carefully as possible. With guns drawn, and using their body armor as a protective cocoon, SWAT members went through the apartment complex floor by floor.

They found nothing.

Then they came upon apartment 523. They saw a busted door and bullet **casings**.

Officer Robot

Ruiz figured Vargas was hiding in the apartment. Ruiz needed to gather as much information as possible, but he didn't want to put his unit in harm's way—yet. He ordered the **deployment** of a four-wheeled robot armed with a camera and a mechanical arm.

The robot was "the eyes of my team," he'd say later. The remote-controlled bot slowly **meandered** into apartment 523 and looked around. Police watched on monitors.

The robot moved through the hallway and stopped before reaching the dining room. Police were shocked at what they saw. The two hostages were squatting on the floor praying.

The male hostage looked up and saw the robot. He used hand signs warning police that Vargas was in the apartment and armed.

A SWAT sniper positioned himself in a near-by building. He couldn't get Vargas in his sights. Police negotiated with Vargas for several agonizing hours. The talks went nowhere.

It was time to move.

It was time to end the standoff.

Later, in the chapter "Mission Accomplished," find out how the SWAT team came through in this situation. First, find out how SWAT teams came to be, along with details about how they do their jobs.

Chapter 1

SWAT officers use military tactics to help defuse situations caused by criminal behavior.

Mission Prep

Many police departments call on SWAT units to handle dangerous situations. Whether it's a hostage case, a bank robbery, a drug raid, or a sniper on a roof, SWAT members are trained to use special weapons and tactics to restore order.

Over the years, SWAT teams have become important units in many law enforcement agencies, including those run by towns, counties, cities, states, and the federal government. Creating a group of officers with special training helps prevent injuries or accidents that might happen if officers were forced to take on challenges they were not ready for. SWAT teams train for months for situations of great danger.

Having a group of specially trained and armed police officers is nothing new for law enforcement. The New York Police Department had one of the first special crime-fighting units in the mid-1880s. Its job was to battle criminal gangs. At the time, police were armed only with wooden nightsticks.

Words to Understand

strategy a careful plan
surplus extra amount
warrant a judicial order giving police specific powers

Over time, however, criminal gangs grew in size. They carried the latest weapons, including machine guns. The gangs became stronger and more dangerous, more than some police units could handle. Police shifted their tactics.

In 1925, the NYPD formed an Emergency Service Unit. The Gunman's Squad was part of the unit. The squad was made up of 60 heavily armed officers. They carried rifles, machine guns, and handguns. They patrolled the streets in green trucks.

As times changed, so did police **strategy**. As criminals grew more brazen, officers found new ways of battling them. The police recruited skilled officers and marksmen and put them in special units. More and more officers began taking fire-arms training and carrying weapons on their daily patrols. Departments began training groups of officers to work together to "raid" criminal hide-outs. Even with that, and despite the creation of these units, police officers still found themselves outgunned. More needed to be done.

The First

In 1964, the Los Angeles Police Department became one of the first to organize a SWAT force. The LAPD SWAT team was originally made up of four units comprising 15 officers. All were volunteers, and most had served in the military. That military experience was important. A police officer's job is to ensure public safety and enforce the law. Police work to prevent crime as often as they investigate it. On the other hand, military personnel are trained in attack and defense. Their goals are to defeat an enemy, not necessarily to arrest them or investigate them.

Among SWAT's first missions in the late 1960s and early 1970s was to confront radical and violent organizations. Two of those groups were the Black Panthers and the Symbionese Liberation Army (SLA). The public was at first skeptical of the new SWAT units. Then two high-profile incidents involving the two groups strengthened public support. The first occurred in 1969. After a four-hour battle with SWAT at Black Panther headquarters in

Los Angeles, the Panthers surrendered to police. The second was in 1974, when an hours-long gun battle left six members of the SLA dead.

The unit also gained fame and support when a television show titled *S.W.A.T.* began airing in 1975. Other cities and dozens of federal agencies soon formed their own SWAT teams.

Growing Presence

The role of SWAT has changed since those early days. Not only do the units confront heavily armed criminals, but they also rescue hostages, battle terrorism, and conduct arrests and searches.

Many of the 18,000 police departments in the United States have SWAT teams. Some have banded together to form regional or state-wide squads. Several U.S. government agencies, including the Federal Bureau of Investigation, the Drug Enforcement Agency, the Bureau of Alcohol Tobacco and Firearms, the Department of Agriculture, and the Fish and Wildlife Service, also have tactical squads.

The number has grown tremendously in recent decades, mostly because the federal government has provided police departments with **surplus** military equipment, including armored cars, machine guns, and night-vision goggles and other gear.

The number of SWAT squads spiked even further after the 2001 terrorist attacks in New York City and Washington, D.C. At the time, the government encouraged local police departments to create their own SWAT squads.

These soldiers from a Navy unit are practicing SWAT procedures.

Calling All Cars

SWAT units have to be ready to roll on a moment's notice. Sometimes they're called to arrest a person on a **warrant** from a judge. SWAT units also serve as bodyguards if a high-profile criminal needs to be transported to jail or to court.

They'll also respond to situations where an armed person barricades himself or herself inside

Sidebar

Expansion

Four years after the 9/11 attacks in 2001, nearly 80 percent of towns with a population between 25,000 and 50,000 people had a SWAT unit. In smaller communities, two out of three police departments formed their own SWAT teams. In the 1980s, SWAT units conducted an average of 3,000 operations a year. That number now tops 50,000.

a building. A SWAT team can end the standoff with an awesome show of power. By working together as a team and using the latest weapons and tactical gear, SWAT teams can overwhelm almost any criminal opponent. That is the biggest change they've brought to law enforcement; the criminals can't outgun the police.

The United States isn't the only country with SWAT units. Many nations, including those in Europe and the Middle East, have their own tactical teams. In France, the national police have RAID teams. Based on the outskirts of Paris, the unit is made up of four ten-person assault groups, all of whom are volunteers. Germany has SWAT teams, as does Great Britain.

The Israeli Border Police have a SWAT unit, the YAMAM, or Special Police. It is mainly used as a counterterrorist force made up of commandos that hunt down suspected terrorists. However,

YAMAM officers perform other SWAT duties, including rescuing hostages and responding to criminals who are heavily armed.

Around the world, special police forces that use military tactics have saved thousands of lives. In the process of that work, a few of the officers who volunteered have also been killed or wounded. Like all peace officers, that is part of the risk they take to do their job and keep people safe.

Text-Dependent Questions

1. How many police departments are in the United States?
2. Describe the difference between strategy and tactics.
3. What U.S. city was the first to form a SWAT squad?

Research Project

Go online and research how SWAT teams work in other countries. Who runs them? How are their tactics the same or different? Can you find a news story that describes an international SWAT operation?

Volunteers help SWAT officers by taking part in training exercises. Here, a SWAT team pulls a "hostage" to safety.

Chapter 2

Training Mind and Body

John Smith was mad—murderously mad. The 18-year-old student from East Bridgewater High School in Bridgewater, Massachusetts, had just broken up with his girlfriend. He decided to let his anger loose on his schoolmates.

As students and faculty piled into the school, Smith **detonated** two homemade pipe bombs. The bombs injured several people. He then shot a school resource officer and a student. Smith then casually walked into the building firing a handgun, leaving a bloody trail in his wake. He ended up barricading himself and several hostages in a classroom. Within moments, the Southeastern Massachusetts Law Enforcement Council's SWAT team arrived, and a standoff began.

Words to Understand

agile nimble or responsive
detonated caused a device to explode
hone sharpen
negotiators people trained to use words, reason, and conversation to reach agreements

The situation lasted more than two hours. It ended well, however. Police talked Smith into surrendering and releasing the hostages. When it was over, police did not arrest Smith. Everyone walked out of the high school alive—even the victims Smith shot. There were no dead bodies. No pipe bombs. Only pools of fake blood and fake injuries. The victims weren't victims at all, just student actors. As for John Smith, he wasn't real, either. He was 16-year-old Brett Harvey, son of the school resource officer.

The make-believe school rampage was part of a SWAT team training exercise. The training day gave police officers a chance to practice their techniques and strategy. Realistic training like this is designed to save lives should the real thing occur. For SWAT officers, the training lets them **hone** decision-making skills and to see what strategies and tactics work in situations that are always changing.

In this training event, some officers provide cover while others rush to aid a victim.

High Stress

Police work is a high-stress job even for the ordinary cop on the beat. Officers do not know what might happen from one minute to the next. Being a member of a SWAT team compounds the stress. SWAT officers know that when they respond to an incident, they are walking into a potential death trap for them, a suspect, or a victim.

That's why SWAT officers are always training. They must be able to think clearly and logically. They need excellent communication skills. They must also be able to solve problems within seconds. They must use their weapons and other gear and equipment with precision.

Lives depend on it.

SWAT officers must be physically fit, **agile**, and good marksmen. Most are pulled from patrol officers who have demonstrated they can handle the physical and mental demands of the job. They must master various technical skills, such as defusing bombs, driving an armored personnel carrier, or maneuvering a robot in and out of tight situations. They must also have an excellent service record. While they do receive additional pay for being part of these units, they don't do it for the money. The officers who volunteer to take on SWAT training know they are taking on a great responsibility and a greater risk to themselves. They make the choice, however, knowing how much good they can do.

Women in SWAT

For decades, SWAT teams were dominated by men. Today, more women are donning the SWAT uniform.

Philadelphia, which has one of the oldest SWAT teams in the United States, recruited two women in 2014. Jasmine Andujar and J'Nean Caserta completed the same rigorous training as their male coworkers. They had to pass a weapons test at a firing range. They also had to drag an adult-sized dummy the length of a football field. The exercise mimicked what might happen if an injured officer needed to be pulled to safety.

In Provo, Utah, Nisha Henderson also made history in 2014. Since the time she was 11 years old, Henderson wanted to be a police officer. She succeeded. When she turned 38, she became a member of the Provo/Orem SWAT squad.

"I would run for miles on the treadmill with all of the SWAT gear on, just to make myself faster," Henderson told a reporter. "Being a SWAT team member has been something that I have always wanted to do. They are the elite—the best of the best. I wanted to be a part of that."

Nisha Henderson says that her story of making the SWAT team can be an inspiration to women and girls to work hard for their dreams.

Variety of Skills

Being part of SWAT is not an easy job. It takes skill, cunning, and brains, along with physical talents. SWAT officers need to learn how to use electronic monitoring equipment that can help them "see" inside a building before they go into action. They must also know the best ways to gain intelligence during a crisis. That might mean talking to the suspect, interviewing witnesses, or researching the building they are entering. They must also be able to battle terrorists and deal with any weapons or bombs they might encounter. Reading up on possible threats and keeping up to date on the latest weapons is part of being a SWAT officer.

SWAT officers are taught to process crime scenes, gather evidence, and conduct interviews with witnesses and suspects. They also provide first aid. Some officers become hostage **negotiators**. That training helps them deal with hostage takers to try to avoid violence. Often, a tense situation can end without gunfire by a trained officer talking a hostage taker into surrendering. Going in with guns blazing is always SWAT's last resort.

Training is grueling. In fact, SWAT units are constantly preparing. It allows them to be mentally sharp, physically fit, and experts in the use of firearms. They run long distances wearing body armor and fire at targets using long rifles, hand-guns, and automatic weapons.

Officers practice in abandoned houses, wooden mazes, and even in computer-simulated environments. They fire at targets while on the move, learning how not to hit a "friendly" target. Some officers train to become explosives and surveillance experts.

On a Raid

All this preparation hopefully will pay off when the call goes out. When SWAT units raid a house or a building, they'll typically move in a single-file line called the "snake." The snake makes it difficult for a gunman to shoot multiple officers, although the officer at the head of the line—the point person, the first to enter a building or a room—is always at risk. The units' mission is to "neutralize" suspects. They have to make life and death decisions in an instant.

Each member of the team has his or her own Area of Responsibility. AORs are designed so

Explosive Breaching

SWAT members often use explosives to enter a suspect's house. It's a tactic called "explosive breaching." A SWAT team's explosive breach team is made up of bomb technicians and veteran SWAT officers. They must know how much explosive to use in a situation. The idea is to move into an area quickly and with complete surprise.

officers don't get in each other's way. Commanders sketch out a plan to show officers where they should focus their attention. The AORs are designed to cover an entire room or an entire building, with each officer's eyes taking one section. SWAT officers have to know all their partners' AORs as well, so they can take over if an officer is hurt. They also look carefully at how they will get back out of a building in case something goes wrong. All of that is communicated to other police officers and emergency workers on the scene. Again, that type of military-like planning and organization is one of the biggest changes SWAT has brought to police work.

Along with officers and their AORs, there are specialists in some SWAT units. Entry specialists are officers who enter a location and rescue a victim. They are trained on many ways to get through locked or blocked doors and how to shield hostages from trouble. SWAT team medics provide medical help for officers and victims. Some SWAT officers are snipers. Their job is to protect victims and other SWAT team members, usually from a distance or a specific location, such as on top of a neighboring building. They also relay critical details that might be needed as a SWAT operation unfolds.

Text-Dependent Questions

1. Describe the role of a breach team.
2. What does a "point person" do?
3. What is the job of an entry specialist during a raid?

Research Project

Research news reports and create a chart that shows the SWAT raids in your community or state over the past year. Categorize each type of raid and the outcome of each incident.

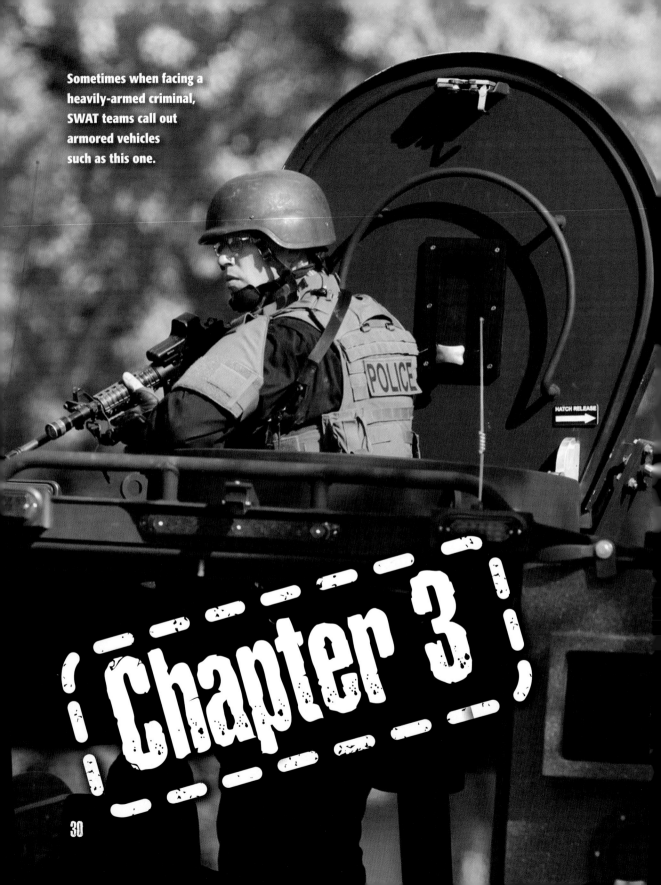

Sometimes when facing a heavily-armed criminal, SWAT teams call out armored vehicles such as this one.

HATCH RELEASE →

Chapter 3

Tools and Technology

Sheriff's deputies in Blackfoot, Idaho, arrived at a local business to contact Scott Phillips. Deputies were looking to serve Phillips with several outstanding warrants. Phillips wasn't having any of it. He barricaded himself in the store where he worked, a produce store on Northeast Main Street. The deputies called for backup. Within moments, the Southeast Idaho SWAT team arrived. They came in two armored vehicles. One looked like a mini tank without the gun turret.

To protect people, police closed off the streets near the business. They set up a command post in the nearby Idaho Potato Museum. Police tried to use a bullhorn to talk to Phillips, who was armed with a loaded weapon and 400 rounds of ammunition. He threatened to harm himself if police got any closer. Police told Phillips to use a cell phone to contact them.

He did.

Words to Understand

ballistic relating to the movement of rockets, bullets, and other projectiles through the air

laser high-powered beam of light

shrapnel metal fragments that scatter when a shell, bomb, or grenade explodes

wield to hold and use a weapon

For 14 hours, Phillips and police negotiated. Finally, police decided to end the standoff. One of the armored carriers busted down the front door of the store. Police stormed in. They arrested Phillips and took him to a psychiatric hospital.

"This is the way it's supposed to work," police officials told reporters. "It's an ideal ending."

The armored vehicle that helped end the standoff was just one piece of equipment SWAT teams use when responding to a call. In addition to these heavyweight vehicles, SWAT teams are equipped with battering rams, stun grenades, protective helmets, body armor, and other gear.

High-Tech Weapons

The weapons SWAT teams use range from automatic assault rifles to semiautomatic pistols to submachine guns. Such weapons are often fitted with flashlights, **laser** sights, and other optical equipment to give officers a distinct advantage.

One of the most important tactical advances in recent years has been "red dot optics"—more commonly referred to as laser sights. Laser sights are mounted on a gun and used by the officer to aim at a target. When an officer sights his or her weapon, a red light appears as a dot on the target. The laser sight allows police officers to keep both eyes open when aiming, giving them a better field of vision. In recent years, thanks to seeing this gear in action on TV and in movies, the red dot has also become a warning to suspects that the police have them in their sights. If a red light can make a suspect give up, that's one less gunshot that has to be fired.

Protective Gear

Helmets, eyewear, body armor—SWAT officers are covered head to toe in protective gear. Although helmets come in many styles, all are military issue. Each is lightweight and can withstand heavy hits.

Eyeglasses are also important. In the old days, SWAT officers wore ski goggles to shield their eyes. Today's eyepieces provide **ballistic** protection. Although the glasses can't stop a bullet, they can protect an officer from flying debris, including metal fragments and other forms of **shrapnel**.

Police departments require all SWAT officers to wear body armor, including ballistic vests. Made of thin, but strong, materials such as Kevlar and covered with canvas, the vests can deflect a bullet or a knife. They are also designed so officers can quickly move from place to place.

SWAT teams pack all the gear they need to do their jobs, from body armor and helmets to weapons and communications gear.

The vests also serve as a toolbox of sorts. Officers can attach other pieces of equipment to the vests, including knives, flashlights, radio handsets, extra ammunition, and other weapons.

Stun Grenades

SWAT police use stun grenades to shock and stagger a suspect. Unlike grenades used by the military in battle, stun grenades are not made to harm anyone. They produce a blinding flash of light and a resounding "bang."

The flash and boom in many stun grenades are caused by an explosion of mercury and magnesium powder. When the grenade flashes, it's like looking into 300,000 brightly lit candles. The sound is as loud as a jet airliner taking off. Both can make a person dizzy and confused. When used correctly, stun grenades, also called flash bangs, let police gain entry into a room by quickly neutralizing any threats. The officers know the bang is coming. They can keep their eyes closed against the light, and earplugs help them deal with the

noise. The suspects don't have that protection…
and they don't know when the bang is coming.

BearCat

When SWAT teams respond to a call, officers often
crowd into the Ballistic Engineered Armored Response
Counterattack Truck, or BearCat for short.
The BearCat is the top of the line in armor-plated
vehicles. Police can use it to control a disorderly
crowd, or to transport a battering ram.

BearCats are four-wheel drive, all-terrain vehicles
that can carry up to ten people. With 15,800
pounds (7,166 kg) of half-inch (1.25 cm) armor,
the BearCat is a high-tech bunker on wheels. Police can drive
right up to a building without
fear of injury.

The vehicle has many uses,
including rescuing hostages and
quelling riots. One model has a
mechanical lift that can reach a
second-story window.

The BearCat provides armored cover for officers in a raid, but it can also be used to transport a large SWAT team to the site of an incident.

Ballistic Shields

Since the days of the ancient Romans and Egyptians, shields have protected humans from weapons, including arrows, rocks, spears, and anything else an enemy might throw at them. In the early days, shields were pieces of carved and chiseled metal. It took a lot of strength to carry and **wield** one. They were effective, although awkward to use.

Today's shields are nothing like the days of old. They come in many styles and can be carried easily. All are bulletproof. In the old days, soldiers had a hard time seeing past the their shields. Modern shields are designed to provide police officers with maximum visibility. Some are even equipped with lights.

One type of shield, a ballistic blast shield, is a portable armored wall. Officers can put it together and move on a suspect with little fear of being injured. Moreover, police can put several together in minutes and build an extended armored

The Tortoise

The idea of combining individual shields to form a wall is not a new one. Roman soldiers knew the tactical value of metal shields. They'd often lock them together over their heads for protection as they marched toward the enemy. It was a formation they called the *testudo*, or "tortoise."

While one officer deploys the shield, another can look around the side to aim at trouble.

wall. Not only does this heavy-duty shield protect against gunfire, but it also can offer protection against rockets, artillery, armor-piercing bullets, and suicide bombs.

Robots

Many times, SWAT teams can't get close enough to a situation to know what's going on. It's too dangerous. When such situations arise, police deploy special robots. The bots are equipped with cameras and microphones. They can be controlled remotely. The robot can walk right up to a situation and get a good view of what is happening. Police also use bots with arms to lift police shields in front of windows to protect officers from a gunman.

One type of robot gives police a distinct tactical advantage when they approach an armed suspect. The SWAT Bot is a portable shield that sits atop a small, tank-like vehicle. The remote-controlled shield protects police as they move into a dangerous area.

The right weapons, the right gear, the right protection…in the right hands: That's how one could describe any SWAT team in action.

Text-Dependent Questions

1. How do flash bang grenades work?
2. Describe the uses of an armored vehicle.
3. How might SWAT teams use ballistic blast shields?

Research Project

Research the types of robots that police departments use. Understand the different functions of each. When your research is complete, create your own police bot using the tools that you think are important. You can draw the robot; create one on a computer, or simply outline on paper what your bot is capable of doing. Share your invention with your class.

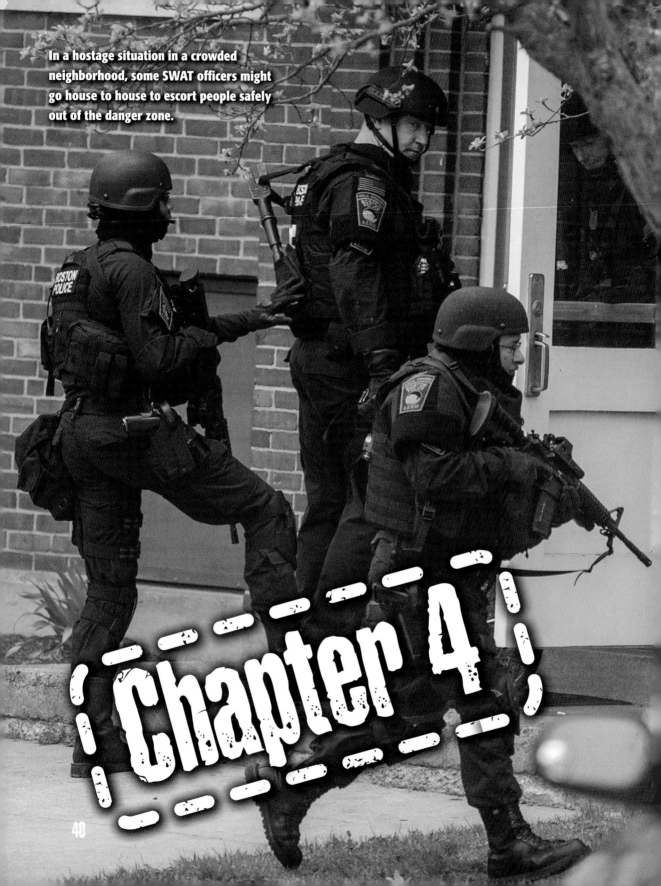

In a hostage situation in a crowded neighborhood, some SWAT officers might go house to house to escort people safely out of the danger zone.

Chapter 4

Mission Accomplished!

At the hostage situation site in Florida, SWAT was on the scene, but it was not quite time to act. The Hialeah SWAT team was poised to move on Pedro Vargas. Its mission was to rescue two hostages without any loss of life. Team members talked to the hostage taker for hours. Nothing worked to get him to give up. Negotiations failed. The time for talk was over.

It was 1:30 A.M.

Six officers gathered in a small group. All were heavily armed. With one minute to go, they huddled and prayed. "We didn't know what was going to happen, but at that moment we only thought of rescuing the couple that had been kidnapped for hours," one team member told the *Miami Herald*.

Words to Understand

disoriented confused
elated happy
poised ready to act

Tough Decision

The decision to send in the team belonged to Police Chief Sergio Velázquez and SWAT Commander Hubert Ruiz. It was one of the hardest decisions of their careers. It would be an all-out assault—a shooting match. No one knew how it would end.

"They are men trained for high-risk situations like this one," Ruiz told the *Miami Herald*. "But they are also parents, human beings I am sending on a mission where they can die."

It had to be done. Such is the job of the SWAT team.

Formed in 1983, the Hialeah Police Department's SWAT team had responded to many situations over the years, but nothing could compare with what they faced during those early morning hours.

The unit is divided into two groups: the Crisis Negotiation Team and the Tactical Team. The negotiation team's job is to end situations peacefully. It did its best, but that was not enough in this case. When negotiations fail, the tactical team takes over.

That's the way it was at 1:30 A.M., when tactical officers began their slow march up to the fifth floor of the apartment building they had under siege. Snipers and other team members had positioned themselves at strategic locations, taking careful aim to protect the men.

The powerful scopes on a SWAT sniper rifle provide an up-close view of the scene. Along with obtaining information, the sniper might be called on to shoot.

Encounter

The police came to apartment 523. They entered the front door and waited in a hallway by the kitchen.

Then, an officer stationed at a nearby building tossed a flash grenade onto the balcony of the apartment.

The grenade exploded in a blistering display of light and noise. The blast caught Vargas by surprise. He was stunned and **disoriented**, but only for a moment.

Vargas was near the dining room. When he came to his senses, he started shooting at his hostages. He was too late. As the grenade went off, the SWAT team had taken those precious seconds to protect the hostages with their shields.

Bullets from Vargas's gun bounced off the armor as the officers covered the hostages with their bodies. A few bullets became embedded deep within the armor. Some ended up in the vests the officers wore. The officers had literally put themselves in the path of a bullet to save lives. Police returned fire. Finally, it was over. The hours-long hostage standoff was at an end. Vargas was dead; the hostages were alive.

"Best Outcome"

"Oh, we were **elated**," said Sergeant Fernando Montalvo, one of the six officers who entered the apartment. "For us, that was the best outcome that we could possibly have. The hostages were super grateful. They were very, very happy, congratulating us, wanting to meet us."

The officers of the Hialeah SWAT team were hailed across the state and nation as heroes. They got a personal congratulation from Florida

Governor Rick Scott. "It can't be easy—you put your lives at risk," the governor told them. "If it wasn't for individuals like you, we wouldn't have the safety we have. I just want to tell you from the bottom of my heart—I want to thank you."

Why did Vargas do what he did? Why did he go on this murderous journey? Why did he confront police, only to die? These were the questions investigators needed to answer. That work began as soon as the SWAT officers made sure the area was safe. As they began putting away their gear, investigators moved in to perform their important jobs.

The work of the investigation would go on, but the important news was that the hostages were safe, thanks to SWAT. "This group is a very united family, but mostly it's a team prepared for extreme situations," Montalvo said.

That family, whether in Florida, another U.S. city, or anywhere in the world, will come together again in an instant . . . ready to use its skills, tactics, and courage to save lives.

Find Out More

Books

Halberstadt, Hans. *SWAT Team: Police Special Weapons and Tactics*. Osceola, Wis.: Motorbooks International, 1994.

Miller, Connie. *SWAT Teams: Armed and Ready*. Mankato, Minn.: Capstone Press, 2008.

Snow, Robert L. *SWAT Teams: Explosive Face-Offs With America's Deadliest Criminals*. Cambridge, Mass.: Perseus Books, 1999.

Whiting, Jim. *U.S. Special Forces: FBI Hostage Rescue & SWAT Teams*. Mankato, Minn.: Creative Paperbacks, 2015.

Web Sites

Bureau of Alcohol, Firearms, and Explosives: Special Response Teams
www.atf.gov/publications/factsheets/factsheet-special-response-teams.html

Federal Bureau of Investigation: Critical Incident Response Group
www.fbi.gov/about-us/cirg/tactical-operations

Los Angeles Police Department: SWAT
www.lapdonline.org/inside_the_lapd/content_basic_view/848

Series Glossary of Key Terms

apprehending capturing and arresting someone who has committed a crime

assassinate kill somebody, especially a political figure

assessment the act of gathering information and making a decision about a particular topic

contraband material that is illegal to possess

cryptography another word for writing in code

deployed put to use, usually in a military or law-enforcement operation

dispatcher a person who announces emergencies over police radio and helps organize the efforts of first responders

elite among the very best; part of a select group of successful experts

evacuated moved to a safe location, away from danger

federal related to the government of the United States, as opposed to the government of an individual state or city

forensic having to do with crime scene evidence

instinctive based on natural impulse and done without instruction

interrogate to question a person as part of an official investigation

Kevlar an extra-tough fabric used in bulletproof vests

search-and-rescue the work of finding survivors after a disaster occurs, or the team that does this work

stabilize make steady or secure; also, in medicine, make a person safe to transport

surveillance the act of watching another person or a place, usually from a hidden location

trauma any physical injury to the body, usually involving bleeding

visa travel permit issued by a government to a citizen for a specific trip

warrant official document that allows the police to do something, such as arrest a person

Index

Photo Credits

Mike Eliason/Santa Barbara County Sheriff's Department: 6, 12, 22, 35, 38; Newscom: Brian Baer/Sacramento Bee 9, Karen T. Borchers/San Jose Mercury News 30, Gary Reyes/San Jose Mercury News 37, John Taggart/Polaris 40; Dreamstime.com: Dariusz Kopestynski 11, Oleg Zabielin 42. U.S. Air Force/Robin C. Creswell: 17; U.S. Navy/Maebel Timoko 20; Courtesy Provo Police, 25.

About the Author

John Perritano is an award-winning journalist, writer, and editor from Southbury, Connecticut, who has written numerous articles and books on a variety of subjects, including science, sports, history, and culture for such publishers as National Geographic, Scholastic, and Time/Life. His articles have appeared on Discovery.com, Popular Mechanics.com, and other magazines and Web sites. He holds a master's degree in American History from Western Connecticut State University.